26

A book of Poetry

Ashley Renee Cunningham

26

By: Ashley Renee Cunningham

ALL RIGHTS RESERVED.

Cover Design by James Hernandez (Jh7)

www.jamesh7.com

Edited By: Derek Campbell

ISBN: **978-0-692-41351-7**

Introduction

Many people have questioned why I decided to name my book 26 and what the significance of that number is for me. The most obvious reason for me is that at the age of 26, I began penning this book. I turned 26 on July 26, 2014, making 26 my golden birthday. I decided to take it past my actual day of birth and make 26 my golden year. I am admittedly not a "completer." I have given up on myself many times in life and didn't pursue things I wanted to do because I was afraid to fail. I decided this year I was going to let that go. I made a promise to myself to complete a personal project, and thus, my poetry book was born. I have been on a journey of becoming a better me this year. It has been tough. I'm a work in progress and constantly trying to become a better person in general. Other than my age currently being 26, many significant things have happened to me involving the number 26. I moved from Tennessee on September 26, 2012, after spending a year there to help take care of my late grandmother. On November 26, 2012, she passed away, which left me completely devastated. Several times a day I tend to look at the clock at exactly 26 minutes after the hour, and very often I tend to lock eyes with my phone, computer, or clock at 7:26 a.m. or p.m. So after much deliberation, I felt 26 would be an appropriate title for my book. This has been a very long time coming! I penned many of these poems when I was 16 years old. Some of my thoughts involving different matters have changed, and some have eerily remained the same. I never thought I would actually publish a poetry book. To be quite honest, I didn't think my words translated well on paper. I always believed that I was only able to touch people through performance. I hope that isn't true. If one person is inspired by one word in this book of poetry, that will be enough for me. After 10 years of being told I need to write a poetry book, I have finally penned it!

To anyone who ever said I could. To my family, my friends, strangers who have hugged me after I performed, my creator for blessing me with the ability to touch people with my words. To the love of my life for being there for me throughout everything. I love you all, and hope you enjoy reading what has taken me a lifetime to create!

BEGINNINGS

When I was around 7 or 8 years old, I believe, I penned my first poem. The truth is I had always had a love of writing, the arts, and poetry. In maybe third grade I wrote my first book. It was for a school competition that I won—or at least, I believe I won. When I was around 9 or 10, I began writing plays that I would have my friends and cousins perform. I could be quite the little tyrant and always had to have things go exactly the way I had played them in my mind's eye, which I'm sure at the very least annoyed them.

In eighth grade I was asked to write a play for black history month, which of course I enlisted all of my friends in, and I used most of "practice time" as a way to get out of class. I still enjoyed it very much and had plenty of arguments with my friends over my tyranny that I still had not grown out of. In high school was when I first performed poetry. I had been writing more frequently, and one summer while visiting my family in Tennessee, I penned quite a powerful piece on some of the negative things affecting the black community and what needs to be done to change it.

My sister Michelle took me to my first open mic at a Borders bookstore, where I was the youngest performer. I was so taken aback by the love I was shown. I believe it was then that I truly fell in love with performing. I was now ready to perform in front of my high school. I was devastated when at the last minute the principal informed me I would not be able to perform at the school assembly due to some of the wording, which I felt needed to be said. I cried that day after school when I confided to my dad about the situation. He encouraged me to change the wording and reminded me how important the poem was and would be to the students at my school. I did. I performed in front of the entire school and a few local reporters. The poem had great reviews. I performed a few other times at my high school, and was assured by my then very popular best friend that I too would now be popular. I wasn't. I think I liked it that way—the anonymity of everyone not knowing who I was, the ability to be the fly on the wall, the observer. This helped me develop as a writer even more. In my senior year of high school I made friends with an assistant teacher who got me into open mics. It was then that I was able to network with more poets and experience more forms of poetry. I believe it was around this time that I also was being encouraged to write a book of poetry. How boring, I thought at the time. My poetry is meant to be performed. No one will be able to feel the emphasis of my words on paper. I was underestimating my reader and my words. Actually, even now I write hoping that at least one person is able to take something from the words I pen.

Without further ado, I invite you to partake in my words, my poetry, my life. Some of it is personal experiences, others are observances, and some are merely stories. All of it is as important to me as the air I breathe. Some were written by memory, others copied from a poetry journal I started long ago, and some newly penned. I hope you enjoy this very personal and very raw part of me. Some parts you very well may have inspired.

Time for Change

Today it seems our young black women are defined not by her
accomplishments or her mind but by the size of her behind
while males are thugs defined by their money
and young girls all aspire to be the next video honeys
where drugs and violence have taken over our streets and
numerous sex partners is becoming as common as going to sleep
where AIDS is soon becoming the leading cause of our death
and our black men rot in jail for murder drugs and theft
where we still reap the effects of our forefathers being enslaved
beaten down with whips and chains
pride snatched away like blood from our veins
forever having to carry the slave masters' last name
as our fathers are becoming nothing more than a monthly check
baby mothers walking around without a man by her side
as her son looks up to the drug dealers with their money and expensive
rides
where we throw around the word nigga like it's something to be proud
the most derogatory name and yet we say it with a smile
given to us to inflict hate and yet we change it around like it's all ok
taking out the ER
and adding an A
what sense does that make it's all the same thing
where we know all of Lil Wayne's lyrics
but can't remember Dr. King's I have a dream
where the streets are taking our young men to drugs and violence
killing each other our youth will soon be forever silenced
where the media teaches our sons it's ok to call our women by derogatory
names
using being young as an excuse to put our women through physical
sexual and emotional abuse

where our sons are in Jordans as our daughters rock the latest Louis
Vuitton but we can barely pay our bills clipping out coupons
where our men are starting to be on the dl spreading stds throughout our
black communities
rather than fess up to who they are
where our sons' only aspirations are to be the next basketball and rap
stars
where our daughters think it's ok if our sons hit them or cheat lie to them
beat them or treat them like meat
as long as they receive the so-called love that they need
where black love is becoming more of a fairytale and less of a reality
all of this we already know
we were forced to reap what someone else sowed
yet there is still hope for this race that was taken from our homes
beaten and raped
forced to learn another culture and forget our own
yet we must educate ourselves on our history on our own
we must first love ourselves before we can anyone else and we must
admit that there is a problem
in order to get help
all of us have potential to elevate
to become something better
something higher
something great
make the decision now we can no longer wait

Time for Change, was the first poem that I performed in high school. I penned this poem when I was sixteen years old, and performed it at a black history assembly at Hillcrest High School. I was nervous, I said what was on my mind at the time, and what a lot of people needed to hear.

A Picture

A picture is supposed to say a thousand words
yet I heard nothing when I listened to yours
why didn't I hear the numerous times you confided in me
his constant lies his infidelities
the many times you thought you could get away
but what you thought was love
forced you to stay
the bruises you tried to hide
the sweaters in the middle of July
the constant tears putting dark circles around your eyes
as I watched your beauty fade, I prayed and prayed and prayed
what everyone thought was the perfect couple
how little they knew of the truth
Dr. Jekyll and Mr. Hyde
one minute he beats you
one broken rib, busted lip, chipped tooth, bleeding internally, broken
nose
the next minute he's standing by your hospital bed with five balloons and
a red rose
but like your picture I did not say a word
I allowed my best friend to be manipulated and controlled
tears welling up in my eyes as I felt the guilt rise
wishing it was me that could have taken your place
If only this didn't have to be your fate maybe we'll meet again someday
in another place

A Picture, was also penned in high school. My class had just finished reading a book on domestic violence, and I knew a lot of young women were going through similar situations at the time. I encourage anyone to leave when they are being abused in any capacity. It is never worth it.

To Kill

She tosses and turns as she mourns her lost
$300 was the cost
starting to regret what she did
she didn't want him so they killed her kid
this unexplainable feeling
so much more than simply being sad
she took her baby's life
cause a boy wasn't ready to be a dad
cause her mama was ashamed of what she'd done
cause her daddy said she was too young to have a son
cause she didn't want people at school to call out her name
cause she didn't want to feel pregnancy pain
cause she thought it was more to lose and so much more to gain
cause she didn't want to take out her belly button ring
cause she didn't want those stretch marks on her otherwise scar-less
body cause she couldn't go nine months without drinking Bacardi
cause she didn't want her baby daddy to leave
cause she couldn't go a week without smoking weed
cause she wouldn't fit into her new size 4 jeans
so many frivolous things
how can it be so easy to take a life
to not think twice of the decision made to have your own seed slain
why must we keep killing our youth
are black lives not as valuable
is $300 really how much we're worth
to kill a baby
before its birth

To Kill, was also penned in high school. At this time I had observed many young women using abortion as a form of birth control. It was disheartening to know that these young girls thought so poorly of themselves, their bodies, and the babies they were carrying.

Your Cool

Excuse me but your cool is showing
maybe your snapback's just a little too tight
or maybe your jeans are fitting a little too right or maybe it's me
but I don't think you need Prada sunglasses at night to see
that your cool is showing
and yea your Benz is nice and the leather feels alright
but do you really need the top back windows down in the dead of winter
time
I mean this is the Chi
and yea I see you have Skype Twitter Facebook and
Insty I'd rather read a book that I'm intrigued in
rather share a conversation in person
seems like you're allowing your cool to get in the way
of everything you want to do and say like did you
really mean to just say swag five times
there's got to be something else on your mind
I'm hoping you have a little more going than what's on the surface
wondering if you know you have a bigger purpose
chains on your neck starting to resemble a noose
showing off your collection of vodka Cristal and Goose
yea your iPad is cool but I'd rather just sit with you
rather stare into your eyes than all your tags to see the price
it really doesn't impress me
and no you cannot touch caress or undress me
and yes your talk is smooth but I can see right through
not sure what you're trying to prove
but I can see your cool
and no it doesn't flatter
in fact I might like you more if you were a little bit fatter
your jeans should not be smaller than mine
I simply just want your time allow me in to get to know more
oh yea and please leave your cool at the door
no corny pickup lines or expensive dinners needed
I'd rather have honesty like when you say something and actually mean
it or when I say something and don't need to repeat it
rather see you in person instead of Skype
and maybe you might want to put away your cool at least for one night
no need to put up a front or be who you think I might possibly want
we may be able to get something going
if not I'll remind you when your cool is showing

Justice

Justice for YOU YOU YOU AND YOU
because if you are a black man in America they just might shoot
because a system cannot fail those it was never meant to protect
because it might be your son or your daughter next
So justice for YOU YOU YOU AND YOU
blank next to the name
because in a few more months it might be you that's slain
when rioting brings about no real change
but it gets hard when every night you are crying and praying
so Justice for YOU YOU YOU AND YOU
because I see the struggle that you are going through
young black man whose life is not valued
seen as a threat in your own country
treated as a criminal in society
no matter your moral values or education
looked to be a menace to half of the Nation
struggling to bring about change
when you feel like you are running in place and
they keep telling you it's not about race when
it's people that look just like you
killed by a cop eager to shoot
so justice for YOU YOU YOU AND YOU
because if you are a black man in America
they just might shoot

I penned this piece as I watched Michael Brown's mother on television. I wrote as I saw people that looked like me, crying and hurting. I cried, and I wrote.

One day, hopefully soon, I'd like to get married and have a family. When I was younger, I use to think that I wasn't good enough to get married. I thought no man would ever want to marry me. I never felt pretty enough, or good enough, or deserving. I kept these thoughts to myself. Sometimes still at 26, I feel like a failure for not being married. I guess I have in a sense allowed the pressures of society or religion, or just simply my own thoughts, to make me feel less than whole, because I am not yet at that part of my life. These next poems are dedicated to love and relationships. The good, the bad, and the ugly.

Love you

No matter how many times you have
given you a million reasons of why you aren't capable
why you aren't deserving
why you haven't earned it
why you aren't worth it
lies you can't stop repeating
insecurities you won't stop believing
the past you won't stop repeating
companionship you won't stop needing
until it becomes as intricate as your own DNA
convincing everyone you have ever loved they have no reason to stay
after all how can you expect anyone to love you
when you can't even love yourself
no self-improvement
or direction
can't even look at your own reflection
not realizing God made you in his own image
that means you are perfection
the enemy can't even form a weapon
against you...but you...you don't even realize your power
or your beauty your wisdom or your strength.
Even when you don't receive it from anyone else
Remember true love dwells within

Last night I dreamt

Where have you been? He asked.

mascara stricken eyes staring into a half-empty glass

Around. I stammered unwilling to meet his glare

frazzled I jumped as he attempted to run his fingers through my hair

Who hurt you? He asked with a knowing glance.

Why? You weren't there when I needed you. I pleaded you.

I screamed your name in and out of pain

I cried for you

I **DIED for you!** his voice shook the room

Was it not enough that I gave my life.

I bled for you

I was nailed for you

yet you turned your back

put others before me

you were supposed to adore me

What is his name? he asked

Turning my wine in the glass I stared ashamed

it doesn't matter they are all the same

Michael, John, Byron, James

You allowed them to degrade you

turned your temple into a shack

ran too many times around the track

and you always end up right back

it's funny how you only call me

when you're hurt

when they have left

and you're left with the flesh

that I blessed

but I still love you

despite how you mistreat me

countless times you leave me

act as though you don't need me

but cut you and you bleed me

I am embedded so deep in your soul

that no matter how many times you run

you could never truly escape

for I am your heaven

I am your embrace

I am that little voice that you've tried so many times to ignore

I am the one who will always love you

no matter how many times

how many lies

how many crimes

how many sins

I forgive

I forgave

I know all of my children

and you have never been the most brave

too afraid to say no

too scared to let go

too frightened to be alone

but don't you realize that no man could ever truly leave you

for I am the only one you need you

act as though I haven't been here from day one

remember you came and saw me after your heart was broken

and as soon as you got yourself together you disappeared

the moment another man whispered in your ear

the second someone told you they loved you

how can you so easily betray me

nothing no one could ever do or say

could sway me to stop loving you daughter

for my love is unconditional

deeper than any ocean or sea

there is something so special between you and me

that no one could ever come between

and I know in the morning you'll think it was all a dream

just remember this one thing

I am the alpha and the omega

the start and the end

I am your mother and your father

your husband and your friend

I am your protector and your provider

shepherd and messiah

Jehovah-Jireh

I will never leave

I will never forsake

I am your mountain, your moon, your stars

your ocean and your sea

he, he was just your lake

so in the morning when you wake

know that I will be there

watching over you

as I have always been

your ocean your moon

your mother your father

your friend

Last Night I Dreamt, is a poem about a young woman who finds herself constantly going down the same path. She is always giving herself to men that don't deserve her, and then when she is left alone, she returns to God. Once she finds herself enamored with a new man, she goes back down the same path. She doesn't value herself or realize that she will never get the love she desires, without honoring and loving herself. In a dream, God reveals himself to her, and lets her know regardless of her mistakes he will always love her.

Is This Love

lips touch lips
fingers touch hips
buttons unbuttoned
zippers unzipped
seconds turn to minutes turn to hours
only two exist
it's like you scratched everyone else on the list
it's like you took my soul with only one kiss
it's like you stole my heart
saving it until you found the perfect time
to tear to shred to rip it apart
heart snatched out of my chest
mouth smothered with kisses until I had no breath
whoever thought that love could make you want to die
but love doesn't make you constantly cry
bleeding inside
love doesn't leave you bloodied busted lip and black eye
bruised rib on the side so no one can see
the black and blue marks that you're leaving on me
love doesn't rape you in the middle of the night
love kisses you on the forehead and tells you goodnight
love doesn't cheat bringing back whatever disease that you get in her
sheets
love doesn't drop you off at the clinic to abort your seed
love does not hate envy or greed
so how the hell can you say that you
love me

Love is a word that is sometimes abused. Some people use it to control others. Be wary of people who say the love you but consistently hurt you. That is not, and will never be love.

Walls

I built a wall so high
the Great Wall of China couldn't compete
climb the Willis Tower and you still couldn't reach me
stronger than the Pyramid of Giza
stretched further than the wall of Berlin
its only purpose to protect me from men
a bomb couldn't destroy it
the strongest earthquake couldn't shake it
And no man could take it, break it or erase it
with each tear I cried another brick was added
my heart got a little colder and I aligned my wall with more soldiers
their sole purpose to ensure that no man could get in
each one having to pay for one man's sins
the heart he left broken was unable to mend
so my soldiers would defend to make sure the pain
that I felt could never be felt again
and then there was you
my soldiers were defenseless
my wall didn't stand a chance
from the very moment my eyes met your glance
so I did what any woman would do as I watched my walls come
tumbling down…I ran, I ran faster than Usain Bolt running for his life
I ran quicker than the player types run from the words husband and wife
I ran until I couldn't catch my breath
I ran until my heart felt like it would beat right out of my chest
and there you were running right behind me
until I slowed down and you were running right beside me
you singlehandedly removed every brick
every inch of pain you replaced with a kiss
my imperfections are many
you love every inch
you took me from zero to ten
gave my heart the chance to truly love again
even though there's a lot at stake I won't
regret the moves I make
even if I get my heart broken
better than to never have a word spoken

I wrote "Walls" for the play Love Jones. I believe this play can relate to many women and men. Sometimes we love hard. We love so hard we feel there is nothing left. We give our absolute all to a person, and then reach deep inside ourselves and give more. Sometimes those relationships end, and badly. When they do, we swear we will never love again. We put up walls, so to speak, to keep anyone who even attempts to love us out. Not again. Not ever again will we allow ourselves to be hurt. We run as far as we can away from this person, and if they are dead set on being with us, this doesn't deter them. They do everything they can to show us they are not the person that hurt us. They jump through hoops and climb over mountains, and we make them. Not for them to prove anything to us, but because we are so busy running we don't realize all they are going through to get to us. Eventually, we realize it. Maybe a friend all but screams at us, "What are you doing? This person loves you completely! Be with them!" Or maybe if we are smart, we stop running. We look at them and realize they are not the person who hurt us—they are different. We decide we are deserving of love. We allow them to love us, and we love them back, and it can be beautiful

She looked like art

Perfection is never what I wanted
Or aimed for
Attempted
Or slaved for
Art is what I was made for
Creativity I bled for
Late-night tears shed for
I want more
Than you could ever offer
Imagine or begin to fathom
To me this isn't just art
It's my passion

Options

Pretty girl probably could have any man that she wanted
two hundred
plus pictures
added weekly
the likes add up
but still she feels empty
yet still she has plenty
of options
she reminds him
fame it blinds him
no longer paying attention
to her mentions
she's far too thrifty
so he buys toys
to keep his little miss pretty
busy
not aware that the stares
she receives are starting to make her weak in the knees
too busy to understand
she needs more than gifts from a man
much too conceited to believe that she will ever leave
or cheat
he thinks that the little bit of effort
he supplies is enough to keep her
warm at night
but the bed grows cold
and so does her heart
she wants to be treated like art
not like something that you can pick and pull apart
or forget oh so quick
she wants a love that burns in your mental
that you can't forget so
you go back each and every night to be sure that it's still there
something that you can't quite put your finger on it
but your thoughts still linger on it
lingers in your taste buds
wakes you up at night
makes you fiend when you can't have it

want to
reach out and grab it
touch it hold it
maybe even mold it
so that others could feel
what it's like
but it could never truly be replicated
there's no prototype
that will ever feel quite
like the love that she desires
it should start fires
and end wars
fester like sores
when you can't grasp it
collapse and gasp for air
you need it
blind until you see it
you dream it
mad when you awaken
cold sweats
it has you shaking
lost until you find it
dead until you taste
nothing in this world could replace
or even come close
haunts you like a ghost
in its pursuit
hanging like a noose
 realize when you get the girl that everyone wants
despite all of her options
she chose you

Very often, men go above and beyond and do everything in their power and more to go after the "trophy," the beautiful woman with brains. She is the one that men lust for. The one that many attempt to get, but she is selective. She decides to be with the man she loves. The man who shows her the world before he has officially obtained her as his mate. She chooses this man. She stays fit, and keeps her mind sharp, and eventually he gets bored. He has won. He obtained the woman that was hard to get. He doesn't want to throw her away because she is still valuable to him. So he spoils her. He does just enough. He buys her things to keep her happy. He has forgotten that she is deeper than trinkets and shiny things. He stops feeding her mind, he neglects her. He pursues other things, be that work, women, fame. He no longer feels the need to obtain her, so he merely "keeps" her. In doing this he forgets to keep her happy. He forgets the effort he put into making her smile. He forgets the things that makes her laugh and cry. He forgets that she is still wanted. He forgets that she doesn't need him. Eventually if he doesn't remember, then she does, that she has options.

In the end of 2011 I had a very rough year. My maternal grandmother and best friend was losing her battle to breast cancer. I wanted to be there with her to help in any way that I could. At the time, I had ended a three-year relationship with the love of my life. He had made mistakes, and I had a very hard time forgiving them. Some nights I would lie awake all night replaying things he had done in the past in my head. It wasn't fair. I had verbally forgiven him, and yet I couldn't get over anything that had transpired in the past. He was a good guy who made mistakes, and I made him pay for it almost every day. It was unhealthy. Around the same time, I started a friendship with a male coworker. He was funny and a good listener, and I enjoyed talking to him. I still loved my ex, but I had very ill feelings towards him as well. On December 31, 2011, I moved from Chicago to Tennessee to help care for my granny. I tried getting her out of the house and talking to her, but she was always too weak and tired. I would still call my ex sometimes because I still had feelings for him. He never wanted the relationship to end, so it was hard for him to talk to me. I found myself confiding in my old coworker more and more. We started a friendship that had many ups and downs. In the end I felt vulnerable, and unhappy with choices I made. The next selection of poems, were written during this very sad and dark part of my life.

I wish

I wish I never freaking met you
Maybe then it would be easier for me to forget you
Maybe then I could get you out of my mental
Cause you were never really mine more like a rental
And now that I've gotten a chance to test drive
I see you were never what I was really into
But you rode kind of nice
Ok you rode really nice
But that was just the intro
Your owner's manual had a lot of missing info
Or maybe I should have read between the fine print
And yea you were fine but that's about it
Ok you also taught me how to ride a stick
And man here I go about to reminisce about
All the times I went for a ride
See you were the one with the leather inside
Navigation always pointed me in the wrong direction
All those other women trying to steal you had me stressing
I should have known that I could never afford you
Though I still bought yo' butt those rims trying to spoil you
wouldn't even let my friends come around you
But somehow some way trouble always found you
Your tinted windows had me blinded
808s in my ear so your voice was the only one that I could ever hear
My momma tried to warn me daddy said you wasn't safe
And a girl like me need something my own pace
But I couldn't slow down
Late nights early mornings
I lived for the sound of your engine roaring
Top back windows down
Felt like I was soaring
Up until the end
When I found all the letters the other girls had penned
When I saw the earrings she left in my car
When I found the shirt, the panties, the bra
When you started breaking down making those muffled sounds
Like someone had let your air out sitting on the ground
When you sat in my driveway crying out for days
When I saw that you would never change your messed up ways
When I gave you a second chance and you messed up again

Sad to say but I felt absolutely no remorse
As I lit a match and watch you burn to a corpse
Wish this didn't have to be your demise
No longer able to tell another woman your lies
At least I can say that my love was true
While you were just a hoopty
pretending to be a Bentley coupe

Despite what most people may think this poem wasn't about any person in particular. I wrote it with the thought of any woman who had ever been hurt or lied to in a relationship. Maybe with the thought of a few ex's in mind as well ;)

3/6/12 an ode to you

This picture is painted all wrong
you can call this my last song
better yet my last poem
dedicated to you
took four long months for my answer to come through
but God opened my eyes can't say you were a wolf in disguise
let me know from the get go
and you were so cutthroat
words cut so deep
thought I might choke
need to light up another
and I don't even smoke
and I don't even know
what you're doing to me
but this shit hurts
makes me feel worse about my actions
guess karma's getting her satisfaction
yea I bet that B is smiling
grinning from ear to ear
feeling like the end is near
I fear I won't be able to take the rejection
coming from my latest obsession
my love and my like
my day and my night
stitch and my knife
my eyes are wide open
when I have the answer
why do I keep searching

Once again, settling for a love less than we give, less than we want, and less than we deserve.

Clichés

They say the grass is always greener on the other side
so I took a trip across town and I tried to find someone to replace
as the grass in my lawn had begun to wither I was gone by the end of
December
do you remember
the night we cried
the night I tried to think of every excuse I could to leave
ignoring your pleas
not willing to stick around to see if once the snow melted I would come
back to town
not allowing our grass to grow
I guess I truly reaped what I sowed
falling in love with a possibility
while ignoring the potential of what I already had
what we could have bloomed to
thinking back to November I still do.
They say everything that happens, happens for a reason
never knew me and you would last for more than one season
and I'm thinking what we had was so ugly and beautiful
regret. I digress, I get stressed thinking of how much I gave
and how much I slaved, and how long I stayed
I pray that this lesson will never be forgotten
never speak ill of someone who once made you smile
even when things got so damn foul
lessons you taught I will past down to my child
Absence makes the heart grow fonder
but absence only made our hearts wander breaking hearts in his path
making them love him
to replace the love he couldn't get from me
too selfish to allow myself to see
the pain I had caused
the day that I left him
they say
if you love someone let them go
but if you truly love them how could you let them leave
and if they truly loved you how couldn't they see
that you cut me and I'd bleed you...as intricate as my own DNA
I need you
I see through every hurt you felt
most of which I caused and I applaud your effort
so much stronger than me though I left I came back

what's meant to be will be
he use to get so mad when I'd say it
thinking my mind was already made up because
if I truly loved him how could I have ever gave up
how could I so freely give away everything we'd built
so many nights I lied to myself
hurt people hurt people
I remember the night she died you came to me and I cried in your arms
even after everything that I'd done you held me
wiping my tears as they fell allowing me to yell and scream
the only one who was always there
how could I have not seen from the beginning
the you and I would have had the perfect ending

Sometimes in life people come in, and you aren't sure if they were meant to be a blessing or a lesson. Sometimes it's the blessing that comes from the lesson.

I have been blessed to have gotten to spend time with some very beautiful people in my life. My grandmother, Willie Mae Burney, who was truly my best friend. I spoke to her almost every day on the phone before going to live with her in her last year of life. She taught me so much about life and was always there for me, no matter how stubborn I was sometimes (I got it from her). She was incredibly independent, she had traveled the world, owned businesses, and raised six beautiful children. She was truly the matriarch of my family, and there is nothing that I wish for more than to be able to spend one more day with her.

My great grandmother, Lenzora, who opened her door up to any and everyone who ever needed a place to stay or a warm meal. She was a very sweet woman. I never heard her yell or even saw her get angry. In her last year of life, I stayed with her in nursing homes and hospitals, because she hated being alone. I love and miss her so much.

Finally, Papa Jody. My boyfriend's father. Jody was an entrepreneur at heart and always had a can-do attitude towards everything in life. He encouraged me in so many ways. I miss him dearly, and I see so much of him in Isaac. The following poems are dedicated to you three. I know you are watching over me.

For Grandma Lenzora

Forever in my heart

I saw a picture of you the other day and smiled
Smiled because I know you are no longer in pain
Smiled because I knew you were watching over me
And smiled because it was all I could do to keep from crying
The tears still came
Like a rainstorm in the spring
I cried until there was nothing left
Then I dried my eyes and I cried again
I tried to remain strong
Sang a song
Did a dance
Anything to keep from crying
But the tears wouldn't stop
I cried when I thought of all the lives you had touched
The many people you opened your heart to your home to
The many people you loaned to
Even if all you had to give was an open hand and your sound advice
I cried when I thought of how God had blessed us by allowing us to have
such a beautiful person in our lives
I cried when I realized nothing I wrote
Could ever do you justice or tell of all you did for me and so many others
over time
Tried to paint a picture
Read a scripture
But nothing could compare
To everything you've done what you've given what you spared
I stopped crying long enough for me to write this
You were the sweetest most beautiful person
I will ever encounter no single person could ever compare to the love
that you shared
Perfect from each follicle of your hair to your toes now when I cry it's
because I know
God couldn't have called a more perfect woman home

A Poem for Papa Jody

Strength is not given
strength is earned
strength is what occurs when you have to fight
strength is the tears shed in the dark of the night
strength is the ability to hold on
even when you feel your world is falling apart
strength is not based on doctors and charts
strength is not physicality's no strength is in the heart

and though you may be struggling
at times the pain is more than you can bear
know that God will never bring you

just to leave you there
he sees every tear you shed
the hurt you endured
the sleepless nights when you wanted to give up
the time you cried out why me
begging for a reason why

but remember the teacher
never gives out the answer in the middle of a test
believe me when you hurt he wept
God is only using you to prove
how magnificent he is when he pulls you through
so in times of stress pain and doubt
just remember God is the answer
God is your strength
God is your way out

Survivors

For my grandmother. I miss you, I love you, your memory shall forever live on in me.

15 27 32 48 61 74 it doesn't matter your age
Black White Hispanic Asian Native American
It doesn't matter your race
32 34 36 38
It doesn't matter your shape or size of your breast
As it ravages through your chest making it hard it to breathe
Tossing and turning making it hard to sleep
Making you sick to your stomach as it spreads
Causing you to scream out in pain as it heads up and down
And around as you shed what once was your crown and glory fingers
running through your hair
or what use to be
breast cancer doesn't care that you were once a beauty queen
Mother daughter sister aunt cousin wife grandmother friend
I admire your strength
you are fighters
even when the disease has you bent on your knees in pain
you rise you triumph you fight
even in your darkest hour you muster up what strength you have left
to smile for your families and tell them it will all be ok
you stay you live you conquer another day
you shed tears of joy sometimes pain
you laugh as your grandchildren try their best to entertain you
not knowing the pain that sustains
you give everything you have left
you remove your womanhood your breast to up your chance of survival
you run for the cause you applaud at your children's recital
you smile at the woman across the street who you know is going through
the exact same thing
you cook you clean you do everything you did before

you fear death is knocking at the door and still you fight
at the doctor's at least once a week praying for a cure
you pour everything out into your husband as you weep in his lap
you swim laps with your daughter at the pool
you hold your newborn baby praying she never gets the disease
you beg and plead she never has to feel your pain
you get caught in the rain you laugh
life is too short to be dreary
you reminisce about your first kiss
you miss a day of work
not because it hurts
but because it doesn't
you never quit
pretty as the pink ribbon I wear to represent you
please know that I will never forget you
grandmother sister mother daughter aunt cousin friend
you are all survivors and when you fight
you fight to win

In 2012 I moved back to Chicago and my ex and I started to rebuild our friendship. On November 26, 2012, my grandmother succumbed to breast cancer and he was there. He held me as I cried in his arms. He watched over me until I fell asleep, and he was there for me in the roughest time of my life. My grandmother loved him, and I know she wanted us to be together. In December we decided to start dating again. We rushed into things. We fought a lot and I picked up unhealthy habits. Somehow we were able to get past this rough patch, and I let these bad habits go. Our bond became tighter, and we grew.

The following poems are poems written during this project. These are my most recent thoughts, ideas, poems, stories…some may fall in the above categories but for me it made the most sense to put them together.

Girl in the mirror

she stares at me
taunts me as I look back
you're a pretender at best she spat
you have everyone fooled
miss goody two shoes
but that's not the real you
they don't know about the lies
the cuts on your wrist
the tears at night
that put you to sleep
the emptiness you hide
the fear you pretend to cast aside
they don't know about the addictions
the need for male attention
the confidence you lack
the need to attract
the loneliness you feel
inner scars that never healed
the ugliness you see
when you look at me
or maybe they do
maybe you're transparent
maybe they see right through
they probably all know the truth
you are a complete and total mess
the you who is constantly stressed
the you who never seemed to fit in
the you who no one calls their best friend
the person who can't quite seem to get right
the one who only he sees at night
the girl with the fear of rejection
who hates the way she looks naked the one who feels she has nothing to

contribute
to society
whose weight fluctuates with each new diet
the one who was told she wasn't good enough
pretty enough smart enough
who gave too much away
the girl who has so many secrets she's ashamed
whose closet is overflowing with old bones
whose credit is destroyed by old loans
who fears she will never be able to buy a home
or feel at home
eternally alone
no matter how many people surround her
the girl who will always be unhappy
no matter how many people crown her
or put her on a pedestal
or give her a ring just to please
or pacify
so despite how much you choose to lie
or hide or deny
I see the real you

Every poem in this book is very personal to me. Even if it doesn't necessarily apply to me, or an experience I have been through. When I wrote this poem, I actually was working on another poem, and everything about it seemed phony. It wasn't genuine. I scratched it. I started writing this one. I cried. Every person on this earth has insecurities. So often we put on a mask for the world and pretend to be what we aren't for acceptance. We all crave acceptance and love. Sometimes we put on masks to gain it. We hope that other people won't see how broken we are. We pray that they can't see the insecurities behind our smiles. Not knowing they are thinking the same thing. We push away those who love us completely and gravitate towards others who don't in hopes of gaining their acceptance. We are constantly searching for something. We ignore what we truly need, and that is self-love. We want everyone else to love us, when at times we don't even love ourselves. I didn't want this poem to end with a happy ending. That's not the way I was feeling. It would have been dishonest. I wanted to be vulnerable. So I was and I cried a lot.

Isaac

You send me
You send me round and around
up and then down
across mountains and valleys
cities and oceans
you take me
places I have never been
just to kiss me
you wish me
the best in everything
I attempt or complete
you see
the good in me
when I'm at my worst
you get mad when I curse
you kiss me when I hurt
you send me
backwards and forwards
I mess up you ignore it
or forgive me
you love me
deeper than at times
I've loved myself
you have been there for me
when I felt there was no one else
you make me laugh at myself
when I'm being too serious
you make me delirious
with joy
laughter fills our home
the only time I feel at home
is when I'm with you
I send you hints to buy me flowers

instead you buy me shoes
you cook for me when I'm tired
fulfill my desires
to you I aspire to be you send me
on roller coaster rides
my stomach flips
and grows tight
I still feel the butterflies
your smile
lights up the room
brighter than the moon
I've never felt
any of it before
you pour
yourself into me
 give your last
you clean up the mess that I can be
no matter how many days
how many nights
how many moons
how many lights
how many hours
or minutes or seconds
that we've spent
you still simply have me
sent

I've had the pleasure of having a phenomenal man in my life. He loves me more than anything in this world and shows me daily. Whenever I feel down for any reason, he is there to pick me up with a smile. Sometimes I feel I don't deserve him. He is simply my moon.

Circles

she loved him
or so she thought
he was heartbroken
and she was there to mend
the pieces I tore apart
she listened
as he confided
she kissed him
as he lied
and told her he felt the same
he was in pain
and she was his doctor
his nurse
she cursed the day she met him
enraged that she let him
so deep into her life
just to go back
to the love that had left
to leave her
holding on to the bags he gave
she prayed
for the pain to end
more than lovers
less than friends
hurt people hurt people
round and round we go
he hurt me
so I hurt him
and he hurt them
both lost friends
hearts manipulated in our path
destruction the aftermath
waiting for the day
we can look back
and laugh

In life you never know how your actions can affect other people. Often when we are hurt, we inadvertently hurt other people. Not because we want to, but because we pull others into our lives when we haven't fully healed. We lie to them. We tell them we love them, simply because we don't want to be alone. We lay next to them, because that is what we are used to doing with the one we love. We give ourselves to them just enough to keep them, but never fully. We allow them to give themselves to us. We warn them, but don't stop them from falling in love. We question ourselves. We try to stop, but it feels good. We like the feeling we get from someone needing us and wanting us. We replace the rejection we feel with love from someone we don't truly love. Eventually we move on. We let the person who has been there for us, who catered to us when we were weak and listened to us as we vented, we let them go. If we are lucky, we find or return to the person we truly love. We hope that the other person can forgive us and try to move on as if we haven't allowed our hurt to hurt someone else.

I've Seen a Rose

I've seen a rose grow in Chicago

And Brooklyn

L.A.

Mississippi

New Orleans

To Atlanta

Alabama

To Memphis

And you might not quite yet get this

but

I've seen a rose grow from concrete

From dirt

From project homes

When there was no food to make a decent meal

From slave ships

to plantations

given scraps she made soul food

nations of beautiful black men

developed in her womb

I've seen a rose

That is gorgeous without the need

Of the media's validation

No need to be crowned America's beauty queen

She's a beautiful black queen

Nefertiti, Cleopatra,

Oshun

I've seen a rose

And I know you have too

She's your mother

Your sister

Daughter

Grandmother

She is you

Each year her beauty grows

Leader in college education

The first woman to walk this earth

You can refer to her as your highness

No need to bring her flowers

Her nation grows diamonds

Her hair sheds gold

Defies gravity

She's no tragedy

Or tragic actress

She's played maids

So she wouldn't have to be one

She's freed slaves

So you wouldn't have to be one

She's fought back

Never ashamed of her black

She is the definition of beauty

In a society that doesn't always see it

Or understand

She has sometimes had to play

The woman and the man

She is the most precious jewel on earth

Deemed as difficult because she

Has had to play tough

Twice as good

Just to be considered good enough

She has fought for everything she has acquired

I admire

Everything you have ever been

Or will be

I saw a rose

And that rose

Bloomed in me

THE END

Ashley Renee Cunningham is a writer, poet, and spoken word artist. Ashley is originally from Chicago and currently resides in Los Angeles, California.

Instagram: *@Ashleyreneepoet*

Email: *ashleyreneepoet@gmail.com*

Website: *www.ashleyreneepoet.com*